STAGE 1

What's Alive?

by Kathleen Weidner Zoehfeld
illustrated by Nadine Bernard Westcott

HarperCollins*Publishers*

The illustrations in this book were done with pen and ink, acrylic, and watercolor
on Arches 140 pound cold press watercolor paper.

Special thanks to Eliza Oursler for her expert advice.

The *Let's-Read-and-Find-Out Science* book series was originated by Dr. Franklyn M. Branley, Astronomer Emeritus and former Chairman of the American Museum–Hayden Planetarium, and was formerly co-edited by him and Dr. Roma Gans, Professor Emeritus of Childhood Education, Teachers College, Columbia University. Text and illustrations for each of the books in the series are checked for accuracy by an expert in the relevant field. For a complete catalog of Let's-Read-and-Find-Out Science books, write to HarperCollins Children's Books, 10 East 53rd Street, New York, NY 10022.

Library of Congress Cataloging-in-Publication Data
Zoehfeld, Kathleen Weidner.
    What's alive? / by Kathleen Weidner Zoehfeld ; illustrated by Nadine Bernard Westcott.
       p.   cm. — (Let's-read-and-find-out science. Stage 1)
    ISBN 0-06-023443-1. — ISBN 0-06-023444-X (lib. bdg.) — ISBN 0-06-445132-1 (pbk.)
    1. Life (Biology)—Juvenile literature.   2. Biology—Juvenile literature.   [1. Life (Biology)   2. Biology.]
I. Westcott, Nadine Bernard, ill.   II. Title.   III. Series.
QH501.Z64   1995   94-11450
577—dc20   CIP
                                                                                                          AC

Typography by Christine Hoffman Casarsa
1   2   3   4   5   6   7   8   9   10
❖
First Edition

What's Alive?

Are you like a cat?

You don't look like a cat.

A cat is furry. It has a long tail and four legs.

You have two legs and no fur. But you can run and jump like a cat.

Are you like a flower or a tree?

You don't look like a flower or a tree.

A tree is tall. Its green leaves grow high up in the air, and its roots grow deep underground.

A flower can have petals of pink or yellow or red. You have no petals, and you won't grow as tall as a tree. But, like a flower and a tree, you are growing.

Are you like a bird?
You don't look like a bird.
A bird flies on feathered wings.
You have no feathers and cannot fly. But a bird, a flower, a cat, a tree, and you are all alike in one important way. You are all alive.

9

Many things are not alive. A stone is not alive. Your tricycle, a book, the swing set, a doll—none of these is alive.

Do you know how to tell if something is a living thing or not?

All living things are alike in certain ways.

All living things need water and food and air.

Living things use water and food and air to give them energy. They need this energy to grow and move.

When a cat is born it is small. It is called a kitten. A kitten gets food from its mother. As the kitten grows bigger, it begins to lap up water and nibble on food from a bowl. It breathes air in and out through its nose. The kitten is alive and growing.

Kittens and cats need food, water, and air to give them energy so they can run and jump and play.

13

A baby bird hatches from an egg. It is called a chick. The chick's mother and father feed it. It breathes air in and out through small holes in its beak. The chick is alive and growing.

Chicks and birds use the energy from food and water and air to fly or hop along the ground.

Birds and cats are animals. You are an animal, too. All animals are living things.

Trees and flowers are also living things. But they are not animals. Trees and flowers are living things called plants.

Plants cannot run or jump or fly. They do not eat or drink or breathe the way you do, or the way a cat does. But they do need water, air, and food. And they can move and grow.

Trees and flowers begin as seeds. When they are still small, trees and flowers are called seedlings.

The seedlings grow roots. Roots take in water and nutrients from the soil.

The seedlings grow leaves. Leaves help plants to breathe in a special way. If you look at the underside of a leaf with a magnifying glass, you will see tiny holes. Plants take in air through these tiny holes.

19

Green leaves also help plants to catch sunlight. Plants use the power of sunlight to make food out of air, water, and nutrients from the soil.

Plants use the food they make to give them energy. The energy helps them move. They do not run or jump, but they grow and grow. They bend their stems and leaves to follow the sun.

20

All animals and all plants are living things.

Anything that never needs food or water or air is not a living thing.

Now you can go exploring!

Walk through your house slowly, then through your backyard or the park. Look carefully at everything you see. Draw pictures of each different thing.

23

When you are finished exploring, look at your pictures and see if you can tell which are living things and which are nonliving. For each picture, ask yourself these questions: Does this thing need food? Does it need water? Does it need air? Can it grow or move all by itself? If the answer to these questions is yes, then that is a living thing.

But what if you find a plant that is brown and dry? It will not grow anymore. It cannot take in water or air. It cannot move, except to blow in the wind. Is that a living thing?

27

What if you find a little bird that has fallen from a tree? It lies very still on the ground. The little bird will never move again. It will not eat or grow again. Is the little bird a living thing?

The dry plant and the little bird are living things that have died. All living things eventually die. That is an important part of being a living thing.

A stone, or other nonliving thing, can never eat or grow. It can never run and jump and play. A nonliving thing cannot die, because it has never been alive.

When you've looked through your pictures, try sorting them into piles of living things and nonliving things. Then separate the pictures of living things into piles for plants and animals.

You can hang the pictures on your wall or bulletin board. Whenever you find anything new, you can ask yourself: Does it need food? Does it need water? Does it need air? Can it grow or move all by itself? Then you can add its picture to your collection.

living

nonliving

plants

animals

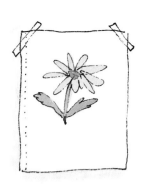

You will always be able to tell what's alive, and what's not.

J
577 Zoehfeld, Kathleen Weidner.
Z
What's alive?